My Love Lives Among The Stars

Amani Carson

To you the reader,
Who has poetry in your heart
And hope running through your veins

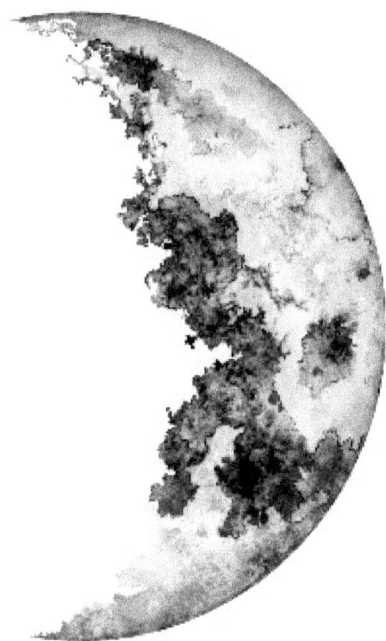

Here's to the love that's not linear. The type of love so intense that you experience it all at once. But that then hides in the gaps of the passages of time, in black holes, lost in the night sky. Only to resurface later on in dreams or in perfume scents or in the melodies of songs.

To the love that could have been but never was. So you keep on replaying it again and again, like a faulty cassette tape. Winding and rewinding, imagining all the possible ways it could have turned out.

To the love you thought you had forgotten about. Until you wake up, years later, in the middle of the night, with the imprint of the person you once knew still burnt into your retinas.

To the love you should have lost but that keeps returning to you. Like the fallen purse handed to you by a breathless stranger. Or the scarf that quietly slipped behind the couch, only for you to find seasons later, untouched and waiting for you to realise that it still belongs to you.

Here's to the type of love that is ever-present. As long as you look among the stars.

My Love Lives Among The Stars

I remember those summer nights I spent alone in my room,
Opening up the skylight for reprieve from the sweltering heat.
The star-pierced, ink-black sky would come into view,
And crumpled notebook pages were strewn across the floor as I
sat,
Jotting down feelings that I had never had.
And there,
Among the strewn leaves of paper and
The candle flames dancing in the breeze,
Like some sort of summertime incantation,
I unknowingly called you into me.

I sat with you that night.

The night was cold, but your smile was warm.

The night was dark, but your eyes lit me up.

Your smile and your laughter;

An innocent beauty.

You laugh and there is nothing else left in the world.

I need to see you again.

I need to make you smile.

Because your pure, momentary happiness

Was infectious in those moments.

I usually fall for brown eyes;
Captivated by their hidden secrets.
Until next thing I know I'm sucked in
Falling into their deepness.

But your eyes were the colour of
The uncharted depths of the ocean.
And that's when I realised
That it's possible
To drown in blue eyes too.

My Love Lives Among The Stars

There were constellations
Burning underneath my skin
And as we touched
They lined up with his

I remember the night I saved you. Your head tilted up towards me, heavy from drink and thoughts and burdens. But your words didn't slur, they spoke softly, gently lulling me into a false sense of security, and travelling to my future self who would keep on replaying that moment. Your eyes weren't watery but bright, if not squinting slightly through the disco lights and dry ice and other elements that kept me hidden from you until that moment. I reached out a hand to help you, like an angel in the night, trying to save a boy I barely knew in a dark bar. And as I walked away, looking back one last time to see a wink and a smile, I knew that I would keep on saving you, time and time again.

My Love Lives Among The Stars

He stood, cigarette dangling from swollen lips,
Leather-clad back leaning against a wall made of brick,
Booted feet nestled on cold cobblestone,
Like some cliché I wonder if my mind once wrote.

But behind his strained eyes was a mind full of lights,
It's spaces filled up with galaxies that shine,
Curious thoughts that bounced between reason and rhyme,
A person not yet burdened by the dead weight of time.

Yet as I stood before him, my eyebrows turned in;
Tired and confused by the rehearsed words I took in.
And only with painful hindsight would I say;
That boy was so much more than a cliché.

My Love Lives Among The Stars

As I waited for you
the sun peaked out from behind the clouds
and birds started to sing
whilst sun rays cast against the ground.
Your beauty
precedes you.

I wanted a love where you couldn't tell if it was real or a dream.

Like you see in movies;

Staying up until dawn

Holding hands, running through the dark

Climbing over barriers and missing the last train

Falling asleep against each other at the station, as we wait for it to

be day

Waking up to soft lips

To the face of an angel

A glowing haze encompassing us,

Accompanying us into the morning light.

I had a love like that once

But the problem with it was

I couldn't tell if it was real

Or just a dream.

My heart nearly imploded,
From all of the things
It wanted to say to you.

I'm having a-million-and-one conversations.
When one leaves from the seat beside me, another appears.
Saying the same lines
I heard a million times that night.

But I've got my eyes on that boy by the bar;
His eyes deep, his lips supple,
Dark hair falling into his face.
His clothes not as uniform as the others trying to impress in this
place.
But his head is turned away, talking to a girl with blonde hair,
Not even glancing in my direction or knowing I'm there.

Later in the night, when I find myself alone,
I spot the blonde girl, whilst the boy has a mind of his own.
She says hello, so I start engaging in polite conversation,
Asking her name, where she's from, what she's doing in this
location,
I ask her what does she do, what does she study, who could she be
And then the boy I had my eye on turns my way and asks;
"Why aren't you asking me?"
I talked to a-million-and-one people that night
And the boy by the bar said

My Love Lives Among The Stars

Why didn't you talk to me?

Remember when you said
What if we kissed
But because I was teased as a child
I took it as just another joke

You pulled me into an embrace
in a crowded room
on a late winter night
and the only sensations I was aware of
were your body against mine
and your snow-laced hair, damp against my skin.

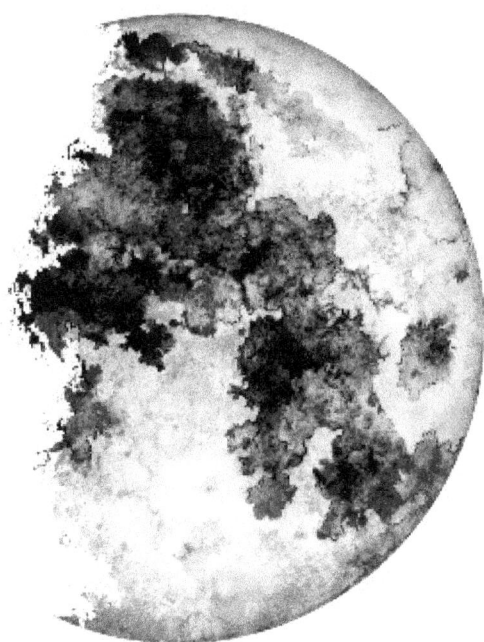

Your heart beat for me.
Each thump of your heart,
A micro piece of poetry.

But the beats were hidden;
Suffocated behind
The bodily cages and confines
Of a love that was forbidden.

My Love Lives Among The Stars

I looked at you
Like you were the moon in the sky.
My eyes wide and open
So I could take in every crevice.
Excited to see if it'd be tonight
That you'd show yourself most fully.
You only came out at night
But you still shone so bright.

You looked at me
Like the sun was in your eyes.
Squinting slightly, like you were unsure what to make of me.
And never looking my way for too long before turning away.
Happy to bask in my warmth,
Without ever getting too close.
Because long ago you learnt that you get burnt
By things that shine.

One night, as part of a university trip
I took a bus into the depths of the wilderness.
The night was alive with sound
As exotic birds flew up above.
And a navy lake lay placid
Whilst stars looked close enough to touch.
As I walked, I wondered what it'd be like experiencing it all with someone,
Somebody whose hands were warm in the night, and their heart full of love.

On the ride back home, as I looked out at the stars that gleam
Someone a seat over to me said,
"Who are you thinking of as you gaze across the stream?"
I laughed and unconvincingly replied, *no one*
That I was just enjoying the scene.

But it was a lie.
As for the whole excursion I was thinking of you.
Because among all the beauty,
I wanted you there, too.

I started writing this letter to you when I was by the sea. But the words were different then. They to-and-froed between optimism and reality, changing like the waves. Filled with a type of melancholy hope that can only be found when watching the tides. In it, I wrote that I hope I won't lose you, but that I fear it's probably already too late. And that also that's my problem, that I never say anything until it's too late. Well I was right, it *was* too late. So I guess this letter is now no more than a bunch of (other) things that I will never say to you.

My Love Lives Among The Stars

If I had a voice
I'd tell you that
I live for your smile
And the light in your eyes.

If I had a voice
I'd tell you that
I've waited so long
For you to be back in my life.

My wildest dreams
Manifested in front of me
And I smile every day.
For my happiness went when you didn't stay.

You're back here with me
But I can't even say,
That I cared for you always
Even when you went away.

If I had a voice
I'd tell you my dreams,
A thousand and one things

For just you and me.

Light to my life,
Fire to my bones,
I don't know what I'd do
If you left me alone.

I go to sleep happy
But wake up so scared,
For I fear for a time
When you won't be there.

I want you to take up
A space by my side,
For you already make up
All the space in my mind.

I want to exist
In the moment with you,
We can make time stand still
I know what to do.

I want to look back
And remember what we had,

If I had a voice
I would tell you all that.

I find you in the strangest places.
In empty streets beneath the trees.
In crowded rooms full of music and strangers.
And sometimes I even find your eyes catch mine
Or your voice say my name.

I find you even when you're not there at all.
In the lines of songs and on the pages of books.
In the caress of my pillow
And in the formation of my smile.

But the strangest place I find you, strangest of all.
Is on my mind.
Constantly and irrevocably.

You are my moon;

You light up the dark places,

You are always in the corner of my mind.

No matter how well things were going between us, I still had this ever-present ball of fear in the back of my mind that I tried so hard not to look at. Because that's the problem with imaginary balls of fear; the more you pay attention to them, the more they grow. Until you can't *help* but look at them. Because now all there is is that thing; a huge, encompassing orb of fear and doubt. My problem is I let that fear grow and grow until it had no other choice but to start existing in reality. Until it took over me fully. A self-fulfilling prophecy made from a fear of loss and anxiety.

How fast
an expression can turn
from one of love and care
to one that looks
straight past you

Isn't it ironic that the ones who tell us
"you should smile more often
'cause you're pretty when you smile"
are the ones who made
our smile a rarity in the first place

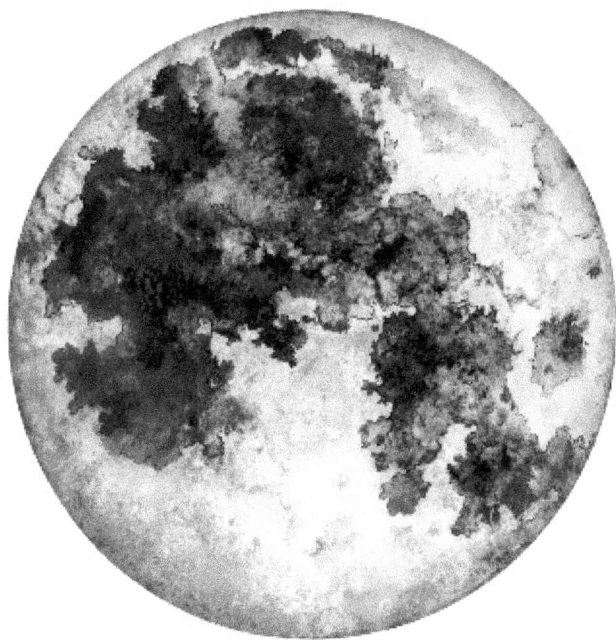

A blood-cold stare

From dark, teal eyes

How can something so painful

Be so beautiful

You broke my heart at the bottom of a staircase,
When I saw you in the light for the first time;
Dark hair brushed away from luminous skin,
Deep eyes the colour of the sea at night,
Full lips not even attempting to grin

You broke my heart at the bottom of a staircase,
When I paused my step, frozen in time,
And when your sunken eyes had lost their shine,
And when your gaze finally turned away from mine

After all the chaos of the night

We stood in the chilly air outside

And your eyes searched mine

And for that moment there was just

You and I

And in your eyes, the colour of a slow dawning night

I recognised

That even if this was the end, we still had something ever lasting

Despite how much it hurt now, I still had that understanding

So I finally pulled away from your gaze for the last time

And looked up at the night sky, willing my tears not to fall

Searching for an answer in the stars

For why everything went so wrong

And when I looked back down to earth you were gone.

I stood with my feet on the sand
Looking out into the ocean
Like it could solve all my problems
As if the future I hoped for was on the other side
If I could only look out far enough

Little did I know
That on the other side
Of the same ocean
You were doing the same
Smiling wide, gazing out at a new future, filled with hope
As you walked along the coastline
Hand in hand
With someone else

Tu me manques. *You are missing from me.* Our ships don't pass each other in the night anymore. I have become an island. Your presence no longer touches me.

You were the light in my life. You filled in all the dark spaces. You lit up the shadows in my world. Without you, the sun doesn't reach my eyes, it doesn't touch my skin. Everything I come across has had its life ripped from it. I can take no joy from my surroundings anymore, they don't touch me. You used to be an aura around me that soaked up all the happiness in the atmosphere and enriched me with it, that protected me were I to fall. The joy doesn't reach me anymore, yet the pain seeps in.

Tears fill my eyes. You are so far from me.

Take my breath away.
Make my heart beat faster.
Make my pupils dilate.

Take my breath away.

Yes, make it harder to breathe.
Make my heart tremble and tweak,
My eyes dampen and gleam.

Take my breath away.

Make me gasp for more air.
Make me call out for help, if there's anyone there.

Take my breath away.

Make my heart painful and weak.
Make me struggle to count the irregular beats.

Take my breath away.

Make my eyes water and stream.

Make them swollen and red and bloodshot from my screams.

Take my breath away.

I wanted you to take my breath away.

Why did I want you to take
my breath away?

Why
did you take
my breath
away?

My Love Lives Among The Stars

In the spring grew our love,
Faster than the blossoms on the trees.

In the summer you were the warmth on my skin,
And the cuts around my knees.

But with the autumn your feelings dwindled,
So our love crumbled like the leaves.

And by the year's end you had left me;
Stranded and cold in the winter breeze.

The night sky was black.
The air cold, my arms empty;
I wanted you there.

I see you, your face
Your hair and its tones,
But you leave me alone.

I once held your grace,
Your skin and your bones,
And all of my woes.

You glance at my eyes.
But I can't conceive
Your words, what they mean.

You walk from my bind,
A smile at your teeth
As you trail with your feet.

The only man who was ever
truly invested in me being okay
was driving the ambulance

Last night I held you under a dreamscape.

Our bodies melded together,

So tight and so close,

Until we both shattered

Into stardust.

You said we were together in an alternate reality. Maybe that's why I stay awake at night, waiting for the house to quiet, for the moon to rise, for the streets to empty outside, the owls to sing, for the stars to dance between the tall trees behind my curtain-less windows, ignoring the heaviness of my eyelids, willing me to slumber. Because as the music from my speakers starts to pleasantly pulsate through my veins and my body becomes airy and light and twilight seeps through the windows I allow myself to think that, yes, maybe we are together in some other reality. And who's to say, with my pillow warm and my lips forming a smile and my eyes now closing softly, that this isn't it.

If I could only go back in time
I would say
Yes.

My life may not be more than a blip on the timeline of infinity.
But so is yours. And ours overlapped.

And to me, nothing feels bigger or more profound than that.

What happens if we meet again? If we close the distance of the years between us?

Will we laugh? Amused to see someone we once knew. Changed after all these years but still somehow the same.

Or will we embrace? Holding onto each other like life itself, until it almost hurts. For how else can we know that it's real this time, and that we won't leave again.

Or will we both look the other way? Because we are different now to the people we once knew. Unrecognisable. Strangers in time.

How can I move on
When you wait there in the dark
Hovering over me while I sleep
Waiting for me to wake in the night to catch a glimpse of you
Like a ghost in the darkness
Haunting me

We can't be apart for long.

I am not complete without you here.

Hi, how are you? Me? I'm doing good. How long has it been? It's so hard to tell. But you look really well.

Hi, how are you? I'm doing alright myself. Some good, some bad. And sometimes work is hell. You know how it is. But it's good to see you again. And I'm glad you're doing well.

Hi, how are you? I'm doing okay but it's been so long since I last saw you that in that time the mountains and oceans stretched out, hiding you away from me with their vast size, and I never thought I'd ever see you again and now that I am it feels like a dream and also like the most real thing that's ever been, I almost feel free, and the sight of your face and the sound of your voice right now is saving me but all I can say is

Hi, how are you?
You look really well.

Maybe we were enemies in a past life.
And our karma in this one is to be inexplicably pulled to each
other
Despite our previous rivalry.
Maybe the universe has a wicked sense of humour
And gave us faces and minds that can't help but be drawn
together.

Yes, maybe we were enemies in a past life.
That would explain all this to-ing and fro-ing
And not knowing how to feel or act so we just keep on going.
All this recycling of these uncomfortable feelings
All the pining and yearning
And the internal bleeding.

Maybe we were enemies in a past life.
And that's why we have all this karma to sort through.
All these messy feelings of love and pain and strife
That we need to sort out just in time
For us to be together in our next life.

I loved you all this time.

We all have little parts of each other that the other person doesn't
have.
Like those lost memories that, when you tell the person, they say
'Oh, I forgot. I can't believe you remembered that.'
I collected those parts of you like trophies.
Like I had this secret version of you when you were with me
That no one else was privy to,
Not even you.
But maybe I mishandled those parts,
Piecing them together like Frankenstein's monster
Until I created someone
Who doesn't exist.

They say that heartache dwindles with time
but as the years go by
I know that even if an eternity passed
I would still be missing you.

I had a dream someone told me you were going to be there.
So then I rushed to touch up my make-up and put a brush
through my hair.
I walked and then ran from room to room
Desperately trying to find you.

It's funny, because in reality
The last time I saw you I avoided you like the plague.
And if someone told me you'd be coming too it would ruin my day
My mind would start flooding.

Yet now in my dreams
I come running.

My Love Lives Among The Stars

They say we like what's bad for us
And that we're helpless to that power
So is that why I crave food that's sweet
And hold on to a love gone sour

69

We created a world in our heads
For both of us to exist together
But the problem is
That even though you're now gone
I still visit it

When I'm going through troubling times
It's like you're deployed into my dreams
Sent from somebody above
To give me a small reprieve.

I don't want any more lovers
Who will rip me apart
Leave me broken
With my heart shattered

I want a lover who
Will patiently stitch up my skin
And hold me so tight that
All my broken pieces
Meld together again

My Love Lives Among The Stars

I have so many things
I never dreamed I would have years ago
so does it really matter
that you're not one of them?

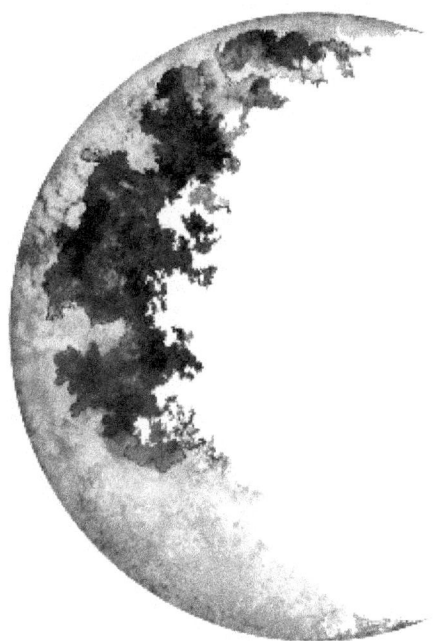

You can't warm your skin
With light from moonbeams
You can't live your life
Waiting on a dream

Leo Rising

I was born after the sun set in the west
When the sun tugged at the moon and the full moon dissipated
When Leo rose in the sky
Giving me a warmth to the tone under my skin,
An edge of fierceness in my doe Libra eyes,
Making me stand tall and lithe,
And making my hair a thick cushion for active thoughts.
But even when my mind is full of doubt
I spend an hour adorning myself to go out
And prefer to love someone made of beauty and style
Even if it means having to wait a while.
But losing something beautiful hurts even more
As does dressing to impress but still feeling invisible
As does having a fierce heart but a tender soul
As does trying so hard yet always having to pick yourself up.
But the definition of courage is trying over and over again
And the fire in me loves surprises
So no matter how many times I fall down
My Leo always rises

As I run out of poems to write about you
I realise that our time together was finite.
And there's no sadder poetry than that;
a notebook that can never be finished.
Empty pages of our story
that will never be written.

What if we don't keep breaking again and again?
What if, instead, we learn to stop at red flags
And learn when to wear armour.
What if we learn to find joy in the small things
And how to cover up in stormy weather.
What if, after everything,
We end up stronger than ever?

It may be scary to think that healing isn't always a linear or one-time thing. But to me there's comfort in the fact that the mind and the body know how to mend themselves over and over. Like how the waves crash against the shore before pulling back again, leaving the bed of sand smooth and fresh, ready to start anew.

I used to love the idea of a twin flame. A person that completes
you. Two people with the same soul.
But somewhere along the line I realised
I don't want to be half-souled anymore.
I don't want a soul that's lonely before it meets you and torn up
when you leave. Ripped out of my body when I grieve.
I want a soul that feels comfy and at home
Inside the warm confines of my body.
A soul that smiles when the sun shines and sighs when I drink
warm tea. That elevates to the sound of music and is comforted
when I read.
I want a soul that's happy and safe and complete
Just being with me.

Sometimes healing comes at the end of your comfort zone. In the moment after you step into the void, after the terror is done tearing apart your synapses. Sometimes healing is the first breath that comes after you survived something every atom of your body told you you couldn't.

When you reach a point of breakdown, you may think you can never get yourself back

but

I've felt the air re-enter my tired lungs when the first notes of my favourite song filled up a concert hall

I've felt the ocean waves that I thought would drown me wash over my body and take away the dark thoughts from my mind

I've seen the smile I didn't know I had reflected on the faces of people I've met, showing me there *is* still joy in me, and that it can merge with the joy of others, expanding into something bigger than fear and sadness.

Maybe next time I'll love someone more tangible and grounded.
Someone who I can hold with my hands and who doesn't slip
through my fingers.
No, they may not have Neptune-coloured eyes
And a mind as expansive as the skies.
They might not have a look so stylish and clean
Or have an aura as luminous as moonbeams.
They may not have lips so pillowy that they raise me higher than
galaxies.
But they'd be warm and solid and present and there.
Yes, next time I'll love someone made of Earth
Instead of sky and air.

As I look out of the window
And watch the dark, winding streets of London skate past
I can almost make out an image of me and somebody,
Walking hand-in-hand along the white townhouse-lined streets.
He'll pull me aside momentarily
Stealing a kiss, thinking no one can see.
My back cold against the brick, but my hands warm from his
jacket's heat.
Then after pulling away with smirks, we'd continue to walk
side-by-side
And the Victorian street lamps would cast our silhouettes against
the pavement lines
And our shadows would be intertwined.

About The Author

Amani Carson is a 31-year-old writer from the UK. Sometimes you'll find her at home in North West London. Other times you may find her halfway across the world. When she's not writing, she spends her time pulling tarot cards and baking gluten-free cupcakes.

My Love Lives Among The Stars is Amani's first poetry collection. In it she chronicles a decade's worth of feeling.

Keep In Touch

Keep in touch with Amani by following her on social media:

Instagram:
@amanicarson
@amanicarsonpoetry

Twitter:
@amanicarson

TikTok:
@amanicarsonpoems

www.ingramcontent.com/pod-product-compliance
Lightning Source LLC
Chambersburg PA
CBHW060035050426
42448CB00012B/3017